People (

Written by Margie Burton, (

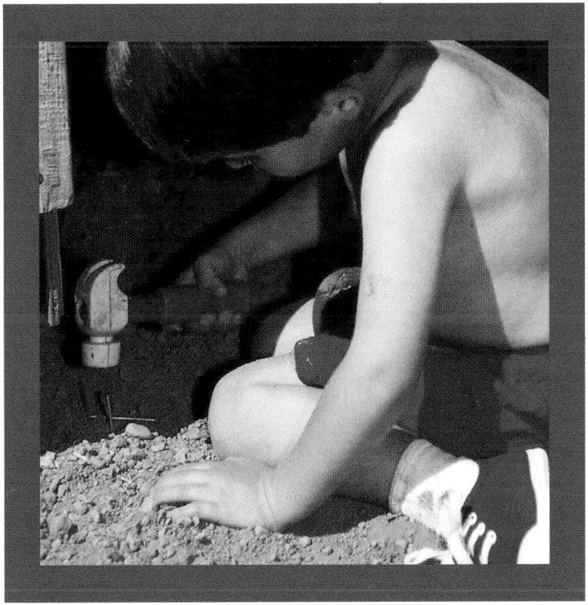

I am looking.

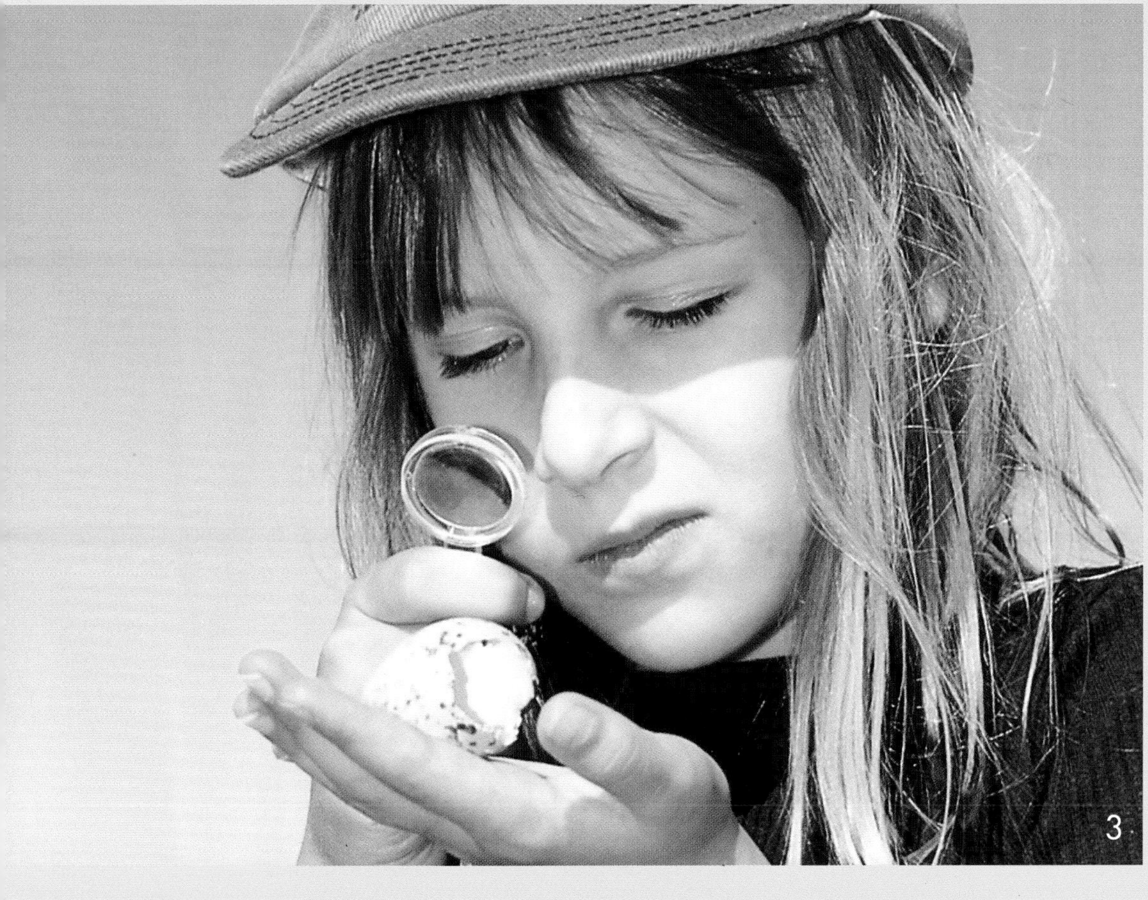

I am raking.

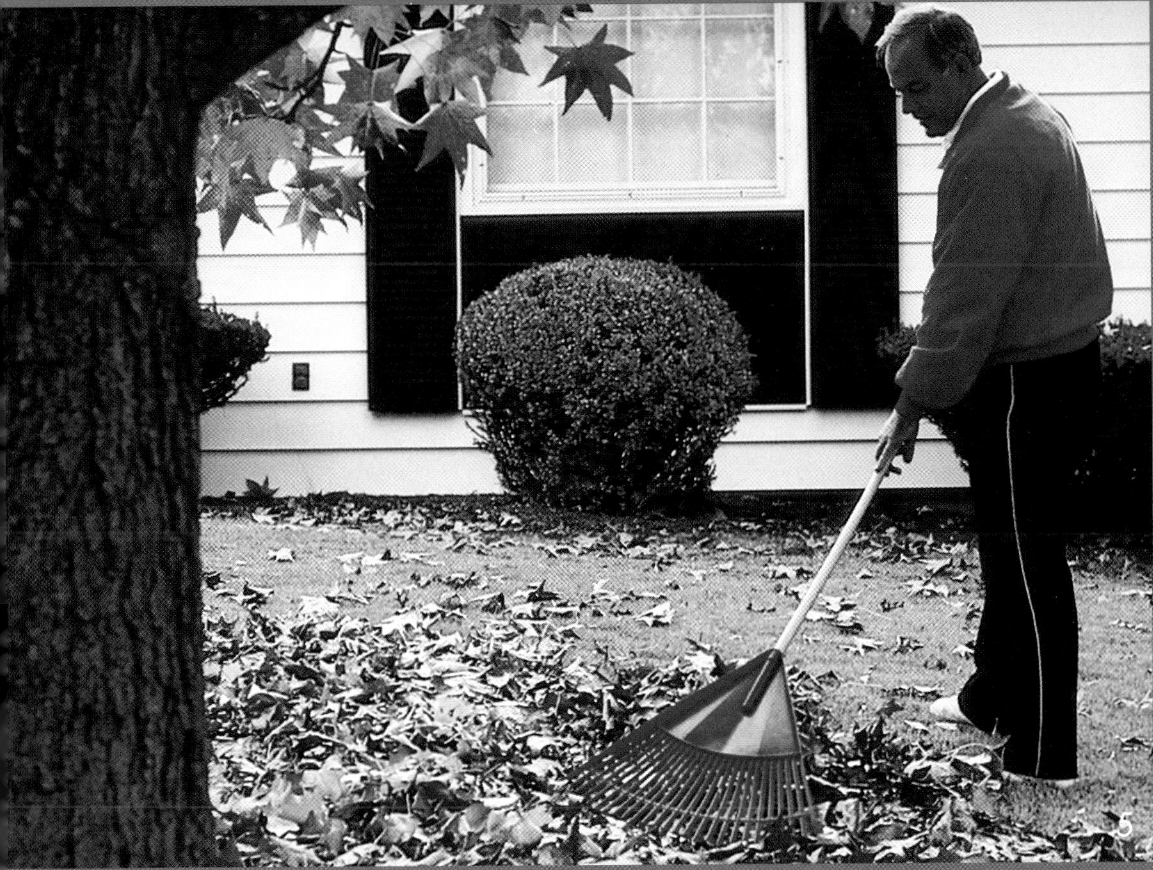

I am cutting.

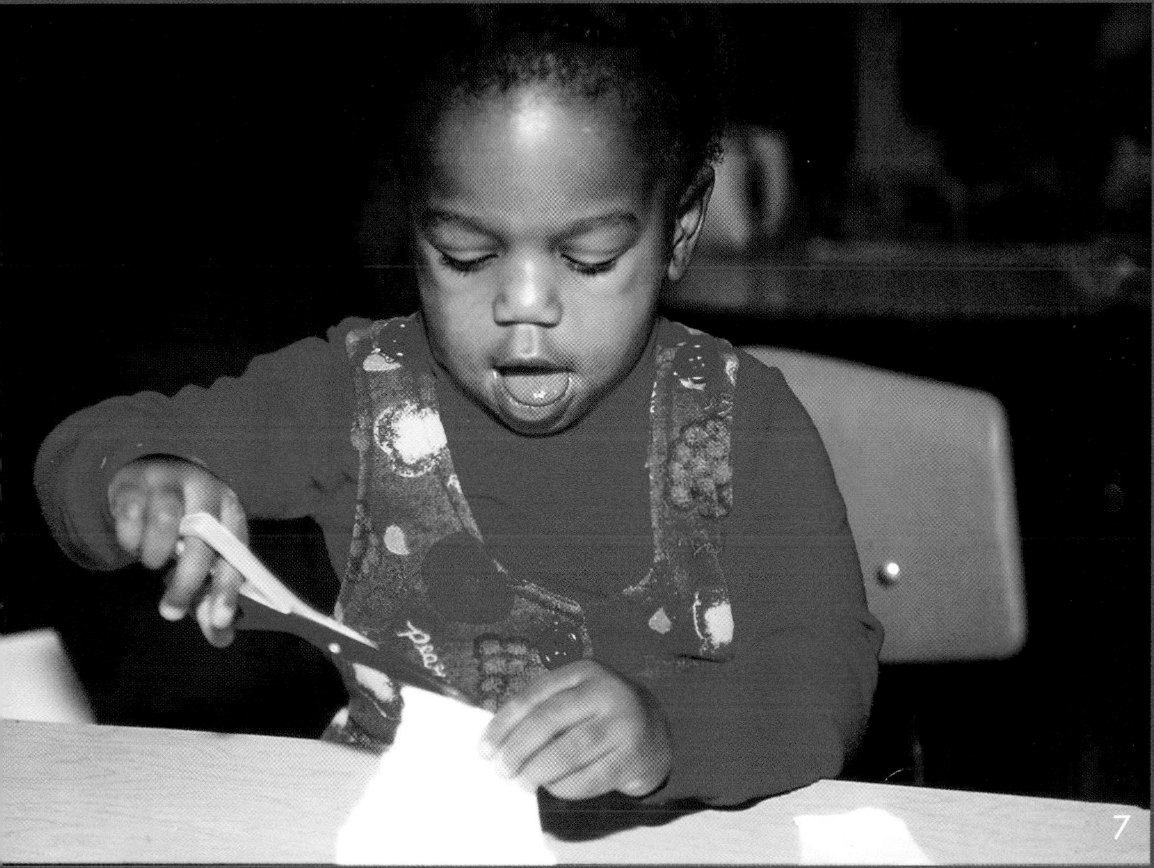

I am writing.

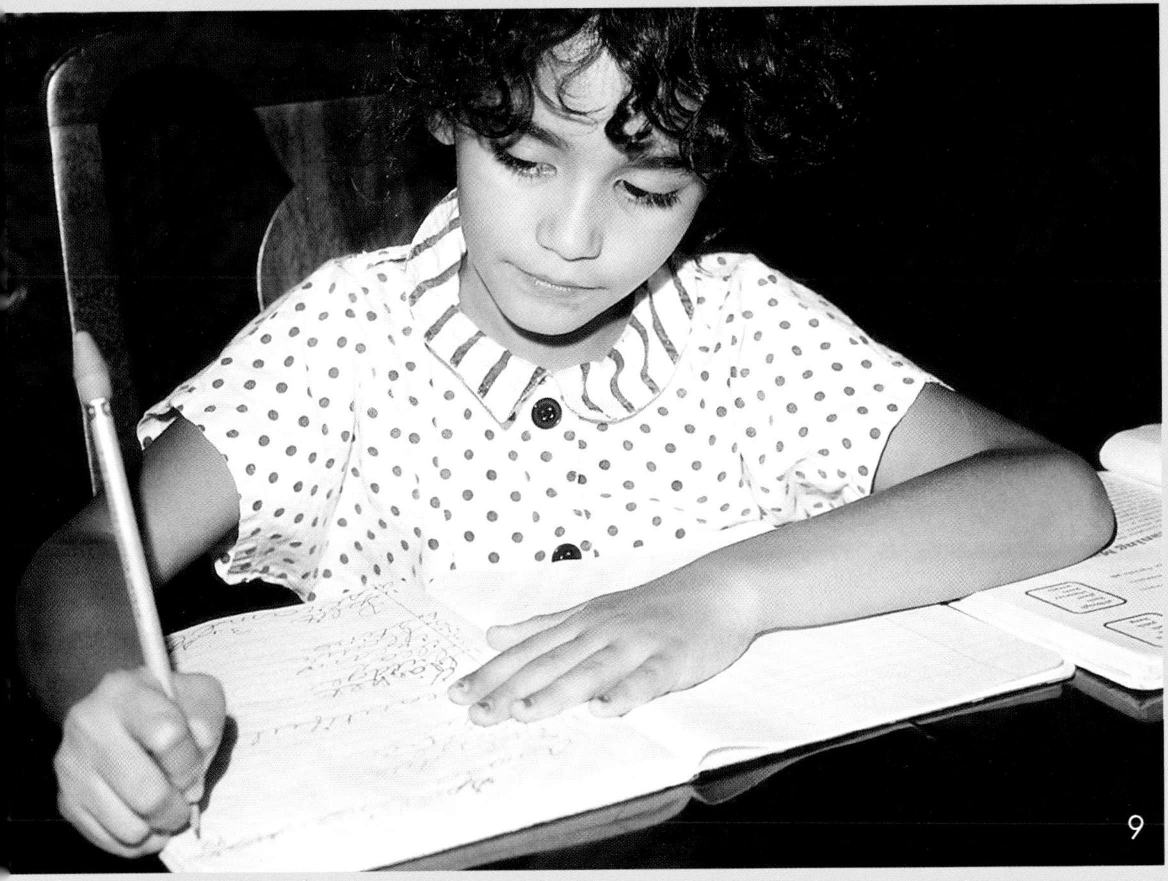

I am painting.

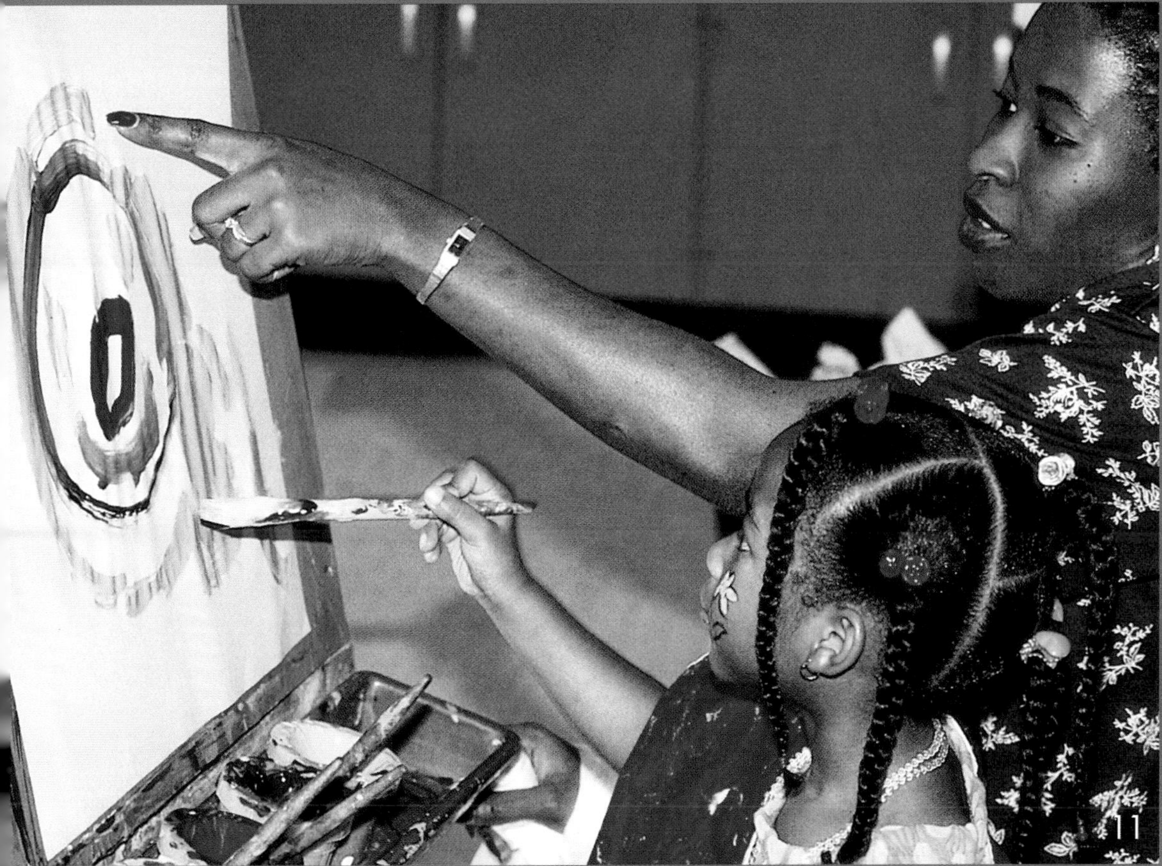

I am cooking.

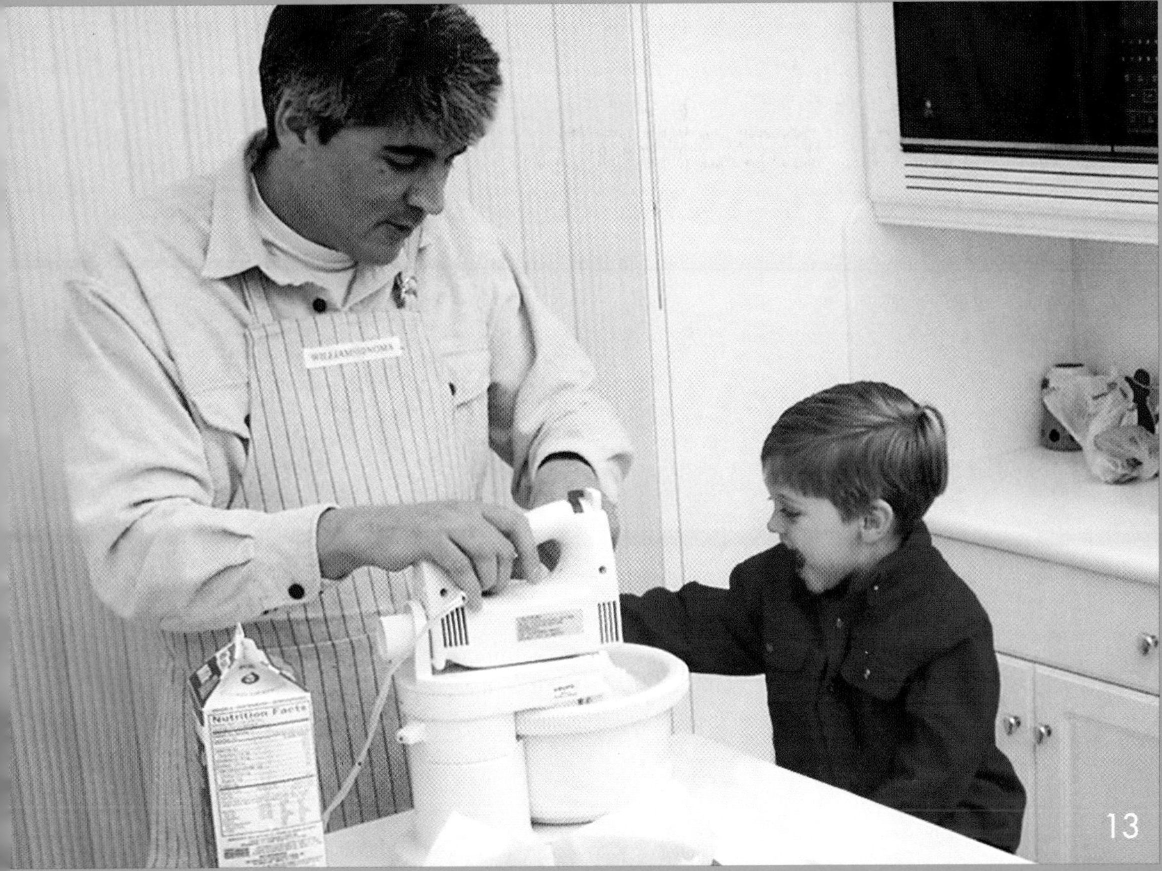
Nutrition Facts

I am measuring.

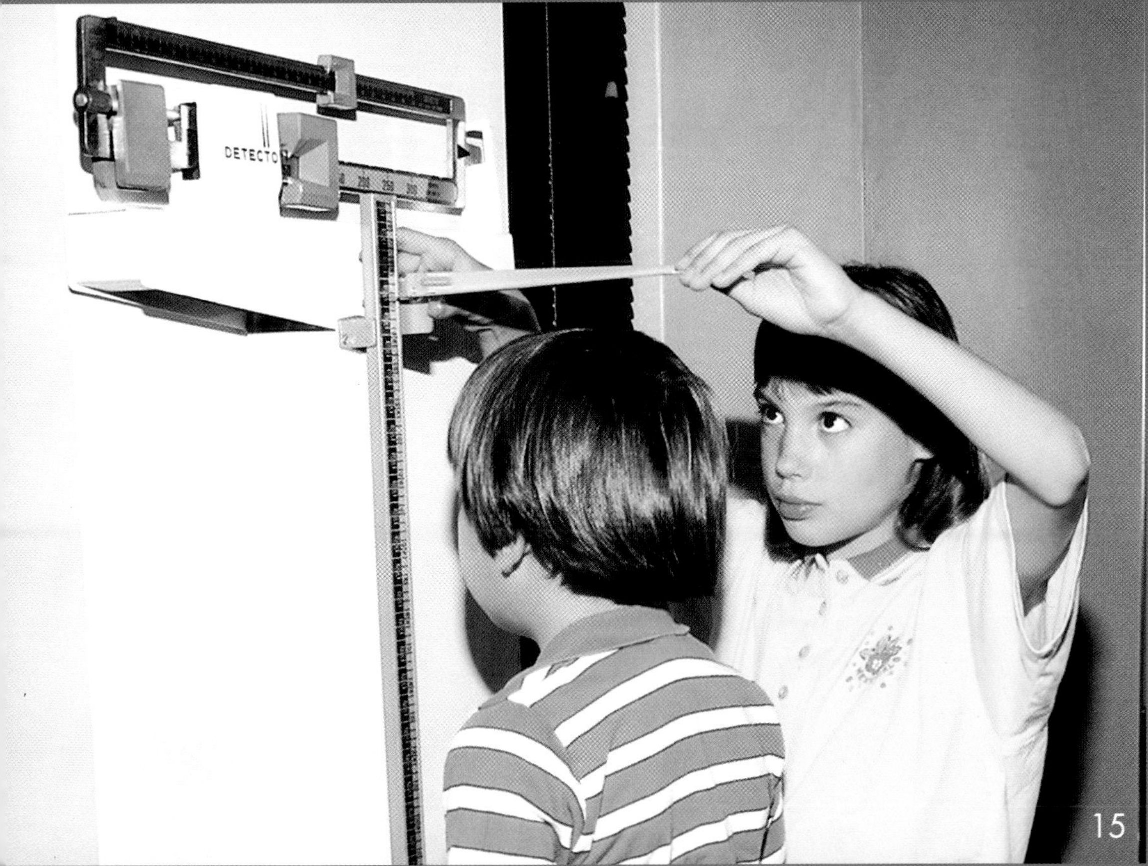
DETECTO

I am weighing.

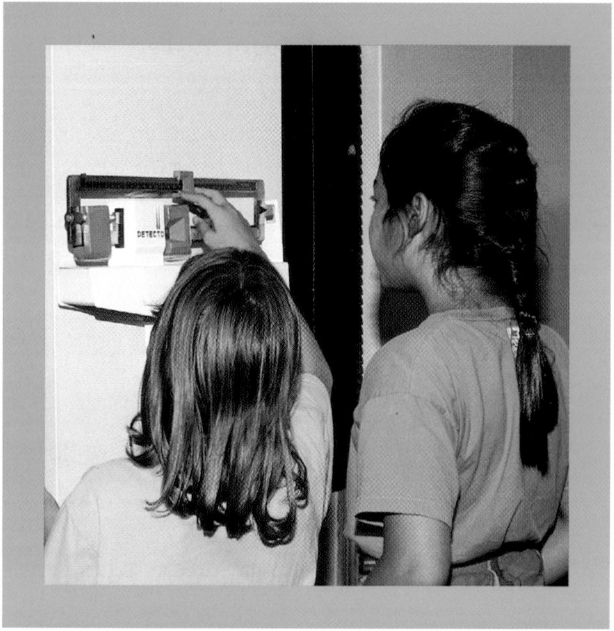